# Black Snow

by
## Bill Garten

authorHOUSE®

AuthorHouse™
1663 Liberty Drive, Suite 200
Bloomington, IN 47403
www.authorhouse.com
Phone: 1-800-839-8640

AuthorHouse™ UK Ltd.
500 Avebury Boulevard
Central Milton Keynes, MK9 2BE
www.authorhouse.co.uk
Phone: 08001974150

First published by AuthorHouse 10/30/2007

ISBN: 978-1-4343-3645-3 (sc)
ISBN: 978-1-4343-3646-0 (hc)

Library of Congress Control Number: 2007907487

Printed in the United States of America
Bloomington, Indiana

This book is printed on acid-free paper.

For my father, Tom and my mother, Wilma

# Contents

# Acknowledgments

*Anathema Review*: "Vacation"
*Antietam Review*: "Frame 142: Before Class"
*Asheville Poetry Review*: "Installment 1005"
*Backcountry*: "Mortalities" and "Complaint"
*Black Bough*: "Frame 160: She Left Us"
*Black Buzzard Review*: "Last Night"
*Blue Unicorn*: "I Got Tired"
*blueLINE*: "Frame 145"
*Bottomfish*: "Putting A Patent"
*Buffalo Bones*: "Frame 63"
*Calliope:* "Frame 751: The Reflection"
*Coffee & Chicory*: "Frame 661: I'm Moving On To Moving"
*Concho River Review*: "Frame 546: That Night"
*California State Poetry Quarterly*: "Frame 1020"
*Connecticut River Review*: "3:00 A.M."
*Cruicible*: "Frame 3000: A White Church"
*Fox Cry*: "Frame 644: Accept It"
*Gambit*: "White"; "Closet"; "Pledge"; "Neglect"; "Riddle"
*Gaslight*: "Frame 655: Lightning Bugs" and "Frame 656: Love Toast"
*Grab-A-Nickel,* reprinted in *West Virginia Arts News*: "At Five"
*Grab-A-Nickel*: "At Twenty-Four" and "Change #1"
*Hawaii Review*: "Frame 1432" and "Frame 1433"
*Iconoclast*: "Frame 253" and "Frame 254"
*Interim*: "Sleeping Over With My Parents"
*Laurel Review*: "Claws"
*Paper Boat*: "Frame 235" and "Frame 237"
*Piedmont Literary Review*: "Child's Nightmare"
*Plucked Chicken #6*: "Recognition #4"
*Poet Lore*: "Frame 323"
*Potomac Review*: "Frame 29"
*Potato Eyes*: "Frame 26: It Is That Time Of Month"
*Pudding Magazine*: "A White Aspirin"
*Raconteur*: "Frame 47"
*Rag Mag*: "Frame 210: Father"
*Rattle:* "As The Road Signs" and "Frame 48"
*Red Owl*: "You Pick"
*S.L.U.G.fest, Ltd.*: "Frame 293"
*Samisda and Wild Sweet Notes*: "At Four"
*Sow's Ear*: "The Blue Cave"
*Stet*: "The Abortion"
*The G.W. Review*: "Frame 50: My Ideas"
*The Wayne Literary Review*: "Infected"
*Timber Creek Review*: "Frame 482A: Breaking Open The Wall"
*What The Mountains Yield,* reprinted in *And Now the Magpie*: "Evenings With Juanita"

# Mortalities

I have died three times in these
Hours they have left me. I have
Cleaned the dishes, the ashtrays,
The crumbs are all swept away.

There in the empty kitchen
Of my thoughts, I brushed away
From my eyes the hair which was
Only a threat or hope it would
Dangle there I have been going

Bald for three years more I am
No longer worried by the wind,
Not afraid of it falling in
On me - like the slow gnawing of
The mouse or whatever it is

That chews away the silence
Of my life as I lie in bed
To forget only at night how
Once I open the curtains
I will see the sleet chipping

Away from the moon and oh how
That light bombards my window
To reflect to reveal to show
I am afraid of this dark
And the sounds of my dying.

# Evenings With Juanita

I drown out kitchen sound with rambling
Piano keys. Foundation lotion, coffee and
Eggs. You fingers skate over my ice skin.
Let me in. Let me in. Scratch my back, dig,

Dig. I call across several states to my old
Philosophy professor, who leaves for Greece
Tomorrow today this beast cries out for the
Touch of your skin. Your fingers are still

Here. Your fingers are gliding. Gliding. I
Undo the knots of your summer cotton dress.
The strings fall lightly behind you. I strum
And chords begin to quiver. Your legs hum.

My thumb. Your pearls. Unknown music.
The white cat yawning on the black leather
Couch next to my red sweater.

# Claws

The girl, who lived here before me,
Got pregnant. Went back home. To
Her parents. In leaving, she left
Her black high heels behind. Coming

Home, in the moonlight, I looked
Down as I turned the key. A black
Starling had been caught by the
White cat next door. The shoes and

The bird. Together. Here. Discarded.
With me on the brick stoop.
I'd been drinking down by the Ohio
Near the flood wall. Got into a

Fight with a river rat from a local
Barge. I smelled like fish from his
Fists. I could feel my eye already
Swollen and black as I opened up.

# White

This thin wall
Where there are no stains
Like my napkin
Still left
Unfolded
On the plastic tray
Never used
During the meal
For there are no
Dinner guests here

Where this
Pale fear
Painted on this
Face
Borders
The starched gown
Probed
Gently
By cold
Fingers

Testing
The stiffness
Of my own
Company.

# The Blue Cave

Hieroglyphics on the inside walls of my heart
Show the story. Tomorrow the archaeologist
Surgeons will try to read the Braille,
What blindly they can't understand, but

Can work on. There is something written.
This much we know. They will do their
Own carving, some sort of new art, in
My secret virgin tomb they will

Invade the years of tribal past and
Drum beating.
When they come to get me, to
Mummify the rest of my body,

I want you to know one thing:
I'm sure my hand will jerk about
Right before I go,
As if the hand wanted so much

To push more rock,
To even rebuild.

# At Four

You took my two brothers to the
Cincinnati Zoo, and left me behind.
You took Mom and the Plymouth
and left me an outer space gun

for a parting gift, as if I lost
on some television game show.
You said I was too young.
The gun hummed and zoomed

and glowed in the dark where I
cried and every morning I shot
the baby sitter knowing at night
while I slept you drove far away

with my family. I dreamed of lions
and bears and seals, when I did
sleep, and when you came back
with photos, I snuck into the closet

at night firing my glow gun. And with
each burst of light I tore the pictures
up one at a time. I knew then I had
bars that one day I would break.

# 3:00 A.M.

The digital dial from the alarm clock
Radio glows like an emerald ember.

Your skin drinks up its blue green light
And your ponytail looks like a giant snake.

The knots in your hair become spiders
Weaving webs out of the strings of light

Bridging shadows of darkness,
You are a sleep drifter, wrapping around me.

# Child's Nightmare

At night
I jar
Fireflies.

Their light
is my fruit.

My mother
Dreams
Downstairs
Of flight.

Above
Still
And
Quiet

I jam
Death.

# A White Aspirin

Melts
On my
Tongue
As I

Watch
A
Perfect
Snowflake

Hit the
Warm
Hood
Of my

Pink
Convertible.

# At Five

I remember
Crawling
Between
Ma & Pa
Late at night
I ran to
Their bed

When thunder
Knocked on
My windows
And lightning
Winked at me

I ran
To the only
Place I
Knew
Where I
Could be
Safe
And warm

Even when
The spot
Between
Ma & Pa
Was cold

I did not
Care
For I was
5 & afraid
Of other
Things
Besides
Failing
Love

# Closet

Gray light
Of mid-evening
Cage
This room

Where I wait
For a
Diagnosis

The nurse
Cleans my
Wound

Closes
The curtains
So I won't
See

Beyond
My own
Disease.

# Frame 26:  It Is That Time Of Month

The full moon is a barrel
Of a gun

A shot is heard
A cerebral safe is cracked

Splattering thoughts on paper
Like a fallen maple leaf stains the sidewalk

A skull is laid open to rest
The squirrel and acorn fall simultaneously

Denting the hood of my car
I lean out the window and scream

At the retarded boy from the next
Farm aiming his rifle

So close to our barn
At night.

# Frame 142: Before Class

I look up and spot
Two planes in the sky.
One refueling the other.
Mating. Leaving a long

White clothesline where
Clouds begin to dry.
In class I am quiet,
Listening to a cricket

Outside in the hall
Walking to the new
Corridor on break
A heavy clumped foot.

Someone's sandals.
Flap. Flap. Like a fan.
Your thighs swishing
In your cotton dress.

The split on the side.
I am back in Saigon.
On leave. Silk. Red.
A dragon tattoo.

Her legs were snow
White. She lit candles
Around me, then

Swallowed the flame.

# The Abortion

From my word
No way for her
To turn back.
Her shadow follows

In every step
But refuses to catch
Her fall.
From my word

No way
To turn back.
Her thoughts float
Buoyed up in a chest

Where a river flows
Downstream.
Down a street
I see her weighing hope

Before the moment
When a sun
Born behind clouds
Buries its bleeding rays,

When a ship sinks
Pardoning its wake.

# Infected

I sit at night while snow flurries scurry outside
I ooze puss poems inside, they refuse to heal.

I put them in a Band-Aid folder as sleep must be
Kept and met like some cocktail party guest.

I throw the staple remover on the brown shag carpet,
It is a prehistoric fish with piranha teeth biting

My toes, paper scarred with type, will not open.
There is no poultice.

# Frame 1020:  All Winter Long

We set separate alarm clocks,
Yours at 6AM and mine at 7:30
In the morning you left with no
Breakfast and I would sleep

Then eat while you drove.
Sometimes at night when you
Fell asleep first, I watched you
And sometimes I wondered

What we lost in that hour and a half
In the morning, like it was something
Incomplete, unrequited, like a bed
That never got made.

# I Got Tired

Of the moving.
At five three times already.
I wet the bed
There was a plant in the
Dining room window
That looked like a wolf's head.
I had to pass that way
To our only bathroom.
So I didn't.
Instead I did it in the bed.
I dreamed of having friends,
But by twelve, we'd moved
Four more times.
By eighteen, three more -

I moved out.

Tonight
My wife came home
Said she got transferred
In the big buy out.
We've been here only
Two years.

I went back to the den,
Started packing my books,
As if they were toys.

I think of the three
Ginkgo trees I planted
Earlier this summer,
The look of my daughters'
Eyes as they peek now
Through the door,
Awakened by the noise.

# Frame 160: She Left Us

All books. She was never able to give
Us all we wanted. She taught us that
We are part of a big Xerox factory.
We are carbon copies of some fig

Leaf manuscript worn and lasting as
Long as waxed fruit. She believed
There was a story in us all. That we
Have total recall. Without therapy.

And that we are all hungry,
Not for company but from it.

# Frame 482A: Breaking Open The Wall

How do I wash this shore of myself?
I can not even see the preview of my
Own movie. Without having some
Fear. Am I the bug that hides when

The light hits this darkness?
The scrambling circle of death
Can not be the same leaf holding
The wind. It is difficult to tell

Who is listening to the sound.
My mother is root bound.
My father is a knot in the trunk.
I am caught in the undertow

Of a dream. Like paying alimony
To the past, the check is bad.

# Frame 50: My Ideas

About myself are gone.
My name helps me remember
Part of it.
The coffee stain on the white

Marble table.
The uncleaned ashes near
My reading chair.

There's a leak in the hall
Mirror
Silver running along
The low side

Where an unplayed piano
Lives on dust.
I know I am a puppet
Catching his own cut strings.

# Last Night

We whistled, played piano, put on
Classical, Country & Western, and Rock n' Roll
You were on the flute later as I danced naked
On the Indian Rug.

We tried but your brand new
Canary would not sing.
Tonight you call me to tell me
The percolator finally brought

Notes to her throat and your
Canary has become a cantor
Over coffee.
As I type this in my old house

The bat, living in the wall next
To the chimney, begins to chirp.
I am serenaded by his fright between
The dead clicks of these keys.

# Frame 644: Accept It

We constantly
Turn to the
Vending machine:
Love.

We plug it
With change
Pulling
The levers

That will deliver
What we hunger
For. But we
Do not find

And we start
Knocking on
The glass and
The metal

And it's empty
The darn thing
Went out of order
Just last week

From pull
After pull.

# Complaint

At breakfast each morning
This week I see the
Way
Milk roller coasts off

Corn flakes
My mind splashes
With thoughts
Of how every

Night I have gazed up
Into that carbon-paper sky,
Where I catch a falling
Star dividing this darkness.

Now I have no pencil
Quite big enough
To connect these remaining
Dots you have left up there

And I know I have no
Right, but
God, that's seven gigantic

Flashbulbs, for one darn picture.

# Frame 3000: A White Church

Trapped by a black iron railing
A lighted night
Pale fingers
Play ivory keys

And black sharps and flats
In a choir room
Music can be heard.
Black notes on

Yellow paper.
A checkerboard embryo.
A belly white turnip.
A hand digging at symbols,

Language and the past.
The mind shovels
Up dirt
And hits water.

# At Twenty-Four

Here in apartment 21
I sleep nights
With a light on
 & A

Winter chill ciphers
Through a crack under
The wooden door.
I think it has blown

Off the dust
There on the small
Book shelf
& the dishes

Are piling up
And they stink from
Mold
But I don't go to

The kitchen
Much
So it isn't so
Noticeable

Yeah, I eat out alot
And took up smoking
And drinking on all
Week-ends

Quit swimming at the "Y"
Gave up oysters
And push-ups -
You probably

Wouldn't like it
Here
At apartment #21
Or me at 24

# Change #1

For twelve years
I glued
Unglued
My muscle arms
To water.
In all that time
My chlorinated,
Blood-shot eyes

Focused on
One black lane line
That ended in a
Cross-like pattern.
Swimming in all
That beer, in all
That smoke.
No. No.

Not one wicked
Incident.
I was clean,
Never drunk
But I got high
Off that conditioning.
Never was I short-winded
Or out of shape,

Until I was All-American.
Such a grand fish,
Such a grand shark
I changed currents
Right into your soft
Soft bed
Panting in that new
Pool of sweat

Now I glue
Unglue
Glue
My strokes to you.

# Pledge

I have the map to
The sea of feelings
But no ship
To carry me

Across those
Foreign waters.
If we take
My wooden heart

And carve
So it will
Buoy up
Among the

Waves,
I promise to let
Your eyes be the
Wind for my sails.

# Neglect

You turn your back
Lying in our bed
Stuck like a
Marble in mud

I glare at you
And can not help
But feel like a
Twig snagged

On a rock
In a stream
Waiting for
A current

To unlatch this
Lock that tightens
Around the edges
Of our love.

# Recognition #4

I have lost
Eighteen
Umbrellas
Successively
This year

When mother
&
I argue
She buys
Me a new
Umbrella

( always with a wooden handle )

Despite
Our altercations
And my
Leaving
Her guilt
In buses
   trains
    and stores

I still
Fear
Being
A son
Caught
In rain.

# Riddle

You breathe a star
You gasp and choke
As its corners
Scrape your lined
Lungs screaming

      your life bleeds

I eat a full moon
Swallowing with a smile
As its edges
Smoothen my throat

      my stomach shines

# Frame 253

Last night the lightning
Took pictures of the windows.
The roll of thunder must have
Been God's indigestion.

You took pictures of me once.
At five, I cried by the railing.
On the front porch. Unable to
Walk as fast as my brothers.

Now I walk across the alley,
Noting broken glass. I empty the trash.
Our house is old and the neighborhood
Full of crime.

You rock back and forth and ask
If I have had my flu shot. If I
Am wearing my hat on cold days.
You are sure it will rain tonight,

Due to the pain in your fingers.
You ask for the family album.
You want to look at photos instead
Of the movie on television. You

Said it moves too quickly.
You can't keep up.

# Frame 254

Love is a spark in the dark.
It glows with air and what
The match and the oxygen know.
Breathing. Blowing.

Words.
What keeps it alive?
Air.
Fanning hands.

What makes it build?
The yearning. Want.
But bright is not
Always to be.

The breath is too
Strong.
The hand
Too quick.

# Frame 63

With brass locks, grandpa's traveling trunk
Lies here like a casket. I have no key.

His picture on top shows each wrinkle,
Bible-soft and running dry. He never smiled.

I now question his facial rivers, rushing
From eyes toward some distant ocean beyond

Cheeks that never felt the dampness of tears.
I have no key. I never will.

# Frame 47

We cuddle under blankets. Listening to rain
And thunder doesn't scare you now as much as
It did before. It's comfortable, this being
Together - we've discovered, there is no doubt.

And the soothing heart beats and our breathing
Dance slowly with the rain and wind. Can we be
Waves gently pounding on each other's shore?
We let each other.

But we are far from any sea.
Without questions or confusion
This joy could never be any other
Way. We are.

I look at you and don't believe for a moment
Any amount of love could be lethal. Before I
Was always too afraid to get too close, for
Fear I'd lose you.

And now I know, as long as I am patient,
Your love, like a prescription,
In the right dosages,
Is a cure.

# Putting A Patent

On hope, I am given the
Room with barred windows.
Here I construct my limbs
In a fold in the

Crevices of a corner.
Here in the tripod clover
Of thought,
Crumpled under pillows

Of flesh,
I soften my jagged world.
I can make my own bed
But instead sleep in

A place not worn by
The wear of light.
In this dusty place
Spiders weave lifeless

Spokes
Coming first to feed.
I bend my chin and
Watch a spider letting go:

Grazing for fine vintage
Air with its sprawling legs
Streaming downward
Until snap -

The carpet catches
The lapse.

# Frame 145

Walking near the river we spotted lights shining,
reflecting, hanging like colored icicles
below the bridges. The rock we had sat and shared
grew cold like our hands. Cigarettes would not warm us

so we shot tequila at a local bar. We still used our
pockets as we skipped home playing leap frog
over parking meters. I thought of how you punished

yourself for what you had refused to do.
You are a river rushing toward someone
else's ocean. I am a cliff listening to echoes
that don't mean anything, but are said

for the sound of it. You asked how we can measure
where we are as we grow. I extend my hand, a catcher's mitt
for fallen stars. Touch your cheek. Tell you to
flow down the river, but never stop.

Once you do you can measure how deep the water is,
but not where or how much you've grown.

# Vacation

Blackbirds speckled the sky,
Dark fireworks that fly.
My eyes keep to two lanes,
Separated by the yellow line.

Reminder: Catch the ebony dots
Fluttering against gray clouds
Take the gamble
So I risk it,

Choosing South for a season.
I have not migrated beyond
West Virginia's mountains for
So long, the control of this wheel,

Capable to turn straight to the
Beach - where I alone will catch
The wind in my hollow eyes,
Like a dead fish, I am washed

Up on my own beach
Of desperation. Going away
From you, I feel on every curve,
My unspread wings.

# Frame 29

Every Spring
I watched the bag lady
Sit daily by Dick's bar.
She read the Sentinel

Sipping from a brown
Bag world.
In the summer heat
She felt above

And beyond
And one day she was
Gone with nothing left
Behind but my memory
Of her and a matchbook

She dropped on the bench
Where she meditated.
Her heart dissolved,
Like a melting Popsicle,

Her thoughts grew sticky,
With no feelings left.
Time, like an army of ants,
Picked her clean.

# Frame 293

From Christmas presents to death,
It's a surprise.
And after we've built
And commit to something

The construction of it all
Was the reason for using
Our tools.
In our new house now

I look in the refrigerator
And realize how
Everything is so
Perishable.

# Frame 210: Father

I never read your book. It remains on a
Shelf, like your love. It stands in a
College library at a school that you and my
Two brothers graduated from. But I didn't

Make a good standing there. You sent me
To learn that there was nothing worth
Learning by tradition. So I left
With my fingerprints on its bindings,

Just removing the dust it hadn't earned.
I was untouched for years by its dedication.
Its title. Sometimes by my own name.
Now I open up one of the few things

You left. Outside of your closed
Casket service, it was your last cover.

# Frame 235

Along the eaten edge,
A new ocean spits its wave on me.
This shore is where I hear the
Music of clothes flapping

On the line
Behind our West Virginia home.
Cabin Creek flooded us out
And in the distance I could

Feel the roar, as father
Turned to catch his skin,
While the wind ripped him away
From himself and my family

Forever I see him turning
And yelling as the waters
Vomited into our valley.
Choking us, pushing us back.

Plastering cows into trees
And house after house served as
A place to catch the spreading
Graffiti

And wrath
That held up against
The old barn
A familiar skull.

# Frame 237

In the bath,
I draw water
Drowning bugs
That hide here

Drain grave
Clean, I come out
Of my apartment
Hole

Like a gopher
Every Spring
To see my shadow
And girls.

# Frame 661: I'm Moving On To Moving

There is an enzyme that plants secrete to kill themselves.
Sometimes when they think they can't grow, they release it.
There is no now, it is gone.

Tomorrow they will saw my sternum open, like some hard log.
My sternum, my shield, didn't shield me from the karate death blow.
My daughter makes popsicles. I want to help her.

The surgeons are wearing a small beacon, like a coal miner's cap
And light. They are mining me.
I told this woman about what the oxygen and match know.

I told this woman what an orgasm felt like for a man. A thousand
Feathered insects running up the shaft of the penis.
I suggested a title for her book of poems. She used it, like my images.

She used me. Stole my ideas. The only thing this will accomplish is
To make me feel better. Someone said I should break into fiction.
I said it wasn't a bank waiting for me. It is a prison when I listen

To other people. I am free writing poetry.
I was born in this same hospital. At three in the morning.
It is forty three years later. It is six in the morning.

I think about all the things I did not do with my daughter.
They are coming for me. These could be my last thoughts
Written down. I'll have others. No one will see them.

# Frame 323

You say you're afraid of driving by the cemetery because
your grandfather is buried there. At six I was afraid to
go by the cemetery because of the Mary Blood curse. So
we're even, sort of. We drive to your only living
grandmother's house. As we move up the Ohio River, by
all the chemical plants, you hold your nose. At the same
time you find beauty in the pillows of smoke coming from
their tall stacks. You say they are dragons. Then you
change your mind and tell me each is God's pipe,
smoking. Each thinking about the river. Twenty-six years
before all this, my parents took me through Nitro, West Virginia
to my grandfather's home. I feared him. Thought he was
contaminated with germs and cursed. It scared me that he
could not play and run like the rest of us. He
Was sick. Dying. Dead.

My father wore sunglasses at his funeral. My brothers,
Joe and Chuck, teased me that grandfather winked at me
as I passed the casket.

This morning when the toast popped up, I saw my
grandfather's face in a piece of bread. I was never fair
to him. I was too scared to love him. Thought I'd catch
something from him and grow instantly old. As I spread
butter on the crisp toast, I remember how mother always
taught me to take the third item back at the grocery
store. She said it was the one least likely to have
been handled by other people carrying germs.

I question if you are growing up with my genetic fears
or somehow you are learning through me. I look at you
and see myself. Your freckles. Your blue eyes. Your
birthmarks, the same ginger color, as mine.

# You Pick

The newly bloomed
Yellow crocuses along the
Edge of the driveway.
I am concerned for you,

My daughter,
So I warn you not to
Pick too many. I ask
Why you have to pick

Them at all. That they
Would live much longer,
Like the memory of
Someone else, I loved,

Who once did
This sort of harvesting.
Like her memory, I tell you,
The crocuses are best left alone.

# Frame 655: Lightning Bugs

Were the stars of meadows when I ran as a child.
With my glass jar, the constellations were snapped
Shut in a capped world. With window sides I held
All the night's light. I was a god. But the illumination

Died off from suffocation. I was careless and forgot
To punch holes. Angry at death, I hurled the translucent
Tomb against the hard trunk of a tree. There my glass
Globe shattered for all time. I bid farewell to the role

Of god, being just a child. Their smashed fate pitched
Any dreams I had across an ebony evening epitaph.
I turned home speechless to realize I was not bleeding,
But I glowed with guilt I could not explain. As a young

Man, I glimpse the stars that are beyond my reach. I am
Glad I keep the fireflies and their enticing beauty at a distance.

# Frame 656: Love Toast

I began toasting the walls of the room,
Giving their pale faces names.
The fifth was half gone and I was hoping
At the bottom I'd find some truth or the

White bunny rabbit my mother used to tell
Me about at the bottom of my bowl, but
Vodka is clear and I see no bushy tail
And the only thing alive in this room

Is a lost moth fluttering up against the
Lamp. A hand grips a gun. A throat drinks
The burn. A tattered moth beats against
A bulb of light, thinking it the moon.

# The Cigarette

Burned the
Persian rug
So this
Brown

Caterpillar
Does not
Crawl
This

Woolly worm
Will not
Predict
Winter weather

But it reminds
Me of the storm
In these lungs
With their

Coughing

Thunder.

# It's Hunger

For warmth
I press

Down
On a piece

Of bread
Fresh

Out of the
Toaster

I reason that
It does not

Matter

Where I get
Love

On cold
December

Nights
I sit

In the kitchen
Feeding

Myself
Madly.

Bill Garten

# Leaves Tiptoe

Up on my green
Patio stage.

They kiss the other
Side of glass doors

That are really hard,
Clear curtains.

Here inside,
Dirty ashes scab

Paper cups, as I
Stare at my summer's

End with stained eyes.
The last three weeks

I've been watching
The sky for the rising

Full moon, tarnished like
A silver coin by clouds

I look for small change,
Thoughts to unhinge

Themselves from the
Skull of me,

White as egg, bleeding
Yellow inside.

# 4997A

The frogs chirp out the
West side of our window.

The fax machine automatically
Receives an incoming message

On the East side of our house.
We can hear its humming as

Paper, like in an old time
Player piano, rolls out.

The sound of the paper
Hitting one by one on the

Cherry hardwood floors
Reminds you of the wind as

It creeps through the screens
Slowly turning the ceiling fans

You think of skin and the
Folding into one another

Like something you would put
In an envelope to keep until

It was ready to mail. Until
It was ready to be opened.

# Dream 97904

I met this young woman with
Jet black hair. She escorted
Me to two mountains where
They mine coal. They were

Huge mountains. We climbed
For a ways, then took a spiral
Shaped elevator up. We had
To balance the elevator with

Our weight and when we shifted
We ended up thrown together
With our arms groping we would
Hold onto one another briefly

Then part. The elevator got to
The top. She took my hand
Leading me across some narrow
Pipes. We were like tightrope

Walkers. I was scared. Wanted
To go back to the elevator.
To go back to the bottom of
The two mountains, but she

Showed me a little of her
Thigh as she turned her leg
She looked at me, pointing
To the end of the narrow

Pipes ahead. There above
The ground, was a perfectly
Made black bed, untouched,
Looking like comfort.

# At Night

I throw the
Army blankets
Up around me
The dust on

The linoleum
Moves like
Small tumbleweed.
At 5:03 in the morning

I hear the bass note of
A coal truck moving
Through the holler
The howls and barks

Of dogs follow. You
Can't hear the birds
At dawn sometimes
The train whistle and

Everything else
Drowns sweet song
Out as I blink my
Eyes open, squeezing

Out the blurring
I see a cockroach
On top of last night's
Beer can

Its antennae slightly
Moving with the cold
Breeze coming under the
Cracks in the dry wall.

# I'm On

The treadmill
Doctor
You are testing
My heart

And I feel like
Sisyphus
With this rock
In my chest

I like the
Mural on the wall
Of the pretty field
It keeps me distracted

With the pain chart
And its different happy
Or sad faces
While I sweat and

Pant, the dandelions
In the green grass
Look like small
Shredded moons.

# They Zapped Me

With the paddles,
They sent their

Electric current
Into my chest

Their lightning life
I am

It is in me here
Surging on my latent

Heart
Rhythm

It grabs what is out
There internalizing it

I see it
Recognize at the right

Cognitive moment
My dormant death

Awakened
I am alive

Dead no longer
On this hospital gurney

Where I was rowing with
My paddles beyond

The edges of my own
Water-skin.

# Aquarium

The first
One

Died
Just

Yesterday.
I looked

All over
For signs

But there
Were none.

So,
I

Changed
The water.

# My Thai Maid

Wipes history off my baby grand as
She mumbles something about the

Scratch, I groan back that it was a
Woman, a fight - nothing.

Months ago you left that small
Signature art in the black wood.

It is an autograph for the eighteen
Months we'd known.

Later this afternoon, I will practice
On the keys, staring into the gleam

Of polish, remembering how smoothly
I once read someone else's music.

Bill Garten

# Sometimes Before Dawn

When the windows are black
When the dark pupils are opening

I feel the peace of where
I've been in

Sleep
Crawls out of us,

On us, like an ant,
Tickling the hairs

Of our leg or arm
We flick off

The day
The night

Yearning not to feel
Gentle dark

Black reminders
Of something

We venture outside
The house

Until we scurry back into
The hole

Sleep
Ourselves.

# Sleeping Over With My Parents

Father, you are a flat guitar string. Bass. Snoring.
Coughing. Sleep picks at you, until you
Are tuned. A heart string. Humming.
Ready to snap.

Mother, you are a wheezing wind, your bronchial
Condition. A horn honks in the alley,
And in your fear, you check through the blinds,
To see if it is the same burglar,

Who in 1946 tried to break in your newlywed
Apartment on Ann Street. After you wash
Your hands for the tenth time,
Your fear gives way to exhaustion.

Dirt and dust dance in your world, so you
Wash the dishes one more time
Before finding the sofa next to the fire.
The wood burning stove is full,

Like me from your cooking. I swallow
Hard. Knowing you are both asleep,
I turn out my light. Freight trains
Couple in the yards just four blocks

Away by the Ohio River. The fan
Clicks, slowly above me. It is winter.
There are no mosquitoes.
I would hear them waiting.

Bill Garten

# Frame 751: The Reflection

Of fenders
In mid-evening
Traffic

Shine within
The gray
Shadows

Of gutters
And down spouts.
Angelic,

The sunlight
Mirrors itself
There in the

Dim darkness
Of houses
Echoing

The oncoming
Traffic and
Tires toiling

The pavement
As snow,
Like chipped paint,

Like white bats
Soaring, spreading
Wings

For the
Flight
Back home.

# He Looked

Into the mirror
But then he took

The mirror
Off the wall

Put it
On the floor

Face up
He jumps

Over the mirror
Jumping

Back and forth
Until he leaves

The room.
The mirror is not

Empty
It just doesn't

Have him in it.
Death's not so difficult.

# Tossed Confetti

These flurries
Look like silver gnats
Swimming in the porch light

I flip off the switch
Staring out the front
Door window

The full moon -
Its light, a gun barrel's end -
Shines down, points at me

The flurries begin to float
Looking like black snow
Beginning to fall

As the wind dies, I breathe in clouds -
My lungs full of cold stars

# Frame 1432

She comes up to me in the bar asking if the stool next to me is taken
and I say no and she says good and she says she has been watching
me as I played pool and I ask her what she is drinking and buy one of
those and she smiles the way dealers sometimes do when playing poker
and she talks and I talk

And she says she wants to go with me and I ask about her history
someone so pretty not necessarily being alone or just broken up and
she says she is married and I recoil like a cue ball when it's hit with a
lot of English and she says not to worry that he has his girl friends and
she has her boy friends and

She wants me to be one of them tonight and I say no thanks I don't
like situations like this and I like myself too much to get into more
pain and she says there is more than one way to get rid of a man and
I feel a little paranoid and she reassures me it is her husband that she
wants to get rid of

That there is this special spice she uses on his dinner that timed just
right should give him a heart attack at fifty and her the house, the kids
and money.

# Frame 1433

I was talking about pubic hair dressing with a woman-poet-friend at this bar and you with your corporate marathon energy stepped up and asked what we were talking about and we invited you to our poetry reading where you sat next to me and you told me later of the electricity the magic you felt and you knew I was the one so you pursued my insecurities my poverty my aloof manner until I agreed after you asked me we would marry and my dad and mom were wondering what happened to me and the wedding was huge with black and white photos in a pleasant November candlelit evening with a Caribbean cruise a new house a new car and cash from your parents and I went from my single apartment to the best section in town and got a great sales job making money and our first and only daughter who is beautiful and when they sliced you open and the crescent moon of blood bore her I knew all the sports trophies all the writing awards were pale compared to this birth this event that led us to more money and a bigger house and another transfer and a nanny who came into our lives to help out and you were away a lot and I started staying up later and one thing led to another and I went to strip bars and drank and started stepping out to poetry readings and meeting people I used to know and more like me and I introduced them to our pool table, our pool, our hot tub and sauna and the next thing I knew I was naked in front of one of them and you are here standing at the bottom of our canopy bed for the first time home early

# Frame 546: That Night

We could
Have sailed
A boat
Across
The Ocean
With your
Sighs

The candle
Bled its wax
Down its
Long body.

You blew
It out
With some
Purpose.

Darkness
Lights
Your nights.

# As The Road Signs

Shadows cross your forehead,
I try to cast my own eyes out
The windshield. Fishing along in
Our car the lights find each

Fluorescent message on each sign
As I look down at you leaning your
Moist mouth against my shirt, my
Shoulder, you sleep.

You, mouth and light are open just
Enough for air to crawl in for you
To breathe part of what you need
And part of your warm breath on me,

As light sculptures your face it keeps
Coming and going from the oncoming
Cars and reflections. I lean over and
Kiss your cheek. I know we are

A hundred miles from anywhere in
This desert, anywhere from being
Safe as I start to pull over to join
You, to forget where darkness

Leads. It is a small failing,
The body, needing rest.
One full of acceptance
When shared.

# Frame 48

Like some
Dandelion

Seed,
I am,

A ghost
Of hope

Moving
Through

The files of
Pollution –

Searching
For ground

I can call
A poem.

Just as I
Get up

Each morning
I, too, kiss

This trick
Glass

Where my
Tongue

Can not
Wash the

Germ
Clean.

# Installment 1005

Gas pains wake him up. Rollins reaches for his
Bottled water by the bed. Aspirin. If they last
Longer than twenty minutes, then call the doctor.
His daughter made him promise. He thinks how
He once grew grapes. How good a glass of wine
Would taste. Veins and vines. How the ivy reaches
Out with its paw-like leaves and stretches, like a
Cat across the patio wall. Yesterday, Rollins ripped

Some off as it ate like a cancer at the mortar
In the sun. Where it grew, there are scratches,
Scars on the red brick. What hieroglyphics
Would look like on an eighty-year old heart,
If it were exposed.
They're the size of a fist, the doctors say.
Our hearts. Rollins thinks perhaps it's really anger
Beating constantly on the inner wall inside each of us.

Nights, like this, Rollins turns more pages.
Effortlessly, his mind races towards the streets
Of his youth. Art. Jazz piano. Talking to women
With such ease, until dawn. He thinks of how
Drunk he used to get, just to anesthetize the
Pain. He questions if there was any love, or
It was just out of convenience, like an alley,
He was too afraid of its trash cans and

Darkness. Too scared to look too far down
To see if it had an end.

# The Absence of Shade

When the sun goes down
The bullets of future
Are loaded in a gun.
Cold and hard and fingered
The darkness is as tight
As any jaw. What can
Bend is what we believe

The bullets of future
Don't weigh much
In the palm that disturbs
Their rest. The color
Of the eye is never reflected
Even when hair is brushed
To one side.

Splendid, the spirit of fingers
Form a window until each hole
In the cylinder is full.
This is where the spin
Of what we leave behind
Gets set in motion,
Where this sun we worship

Lays down on the ocean bed.
On the horizon everything is a yellow sheet,
A sudden flash.

# Black Snow

Waking. This is the start. Eyes read rules.
Thoughts roll like dice. Fingers play
With sharp razor blinds.

Sunlight interrupts dreams
And sound kisses ears.
This challenge of turning a shirt

Inside out, pulled over your head
And there is the hurry
Of ripping sleep

Off passionately
As an erect idea
Divulges there is something

More to do than rent
Reality. There is a need,
A must

If the black snow,
My own sweet sleep,
Is to be believed.

# Box Of Fear

It is not a casket but a box we are buried alive in
While living we walk around in it afraid to take a peek
So we don't look we just avoid it since it is filled
With pain, fear and trauma - an assorted mix of snacks

We really have trouble stomaching. So we leave it
Alone until we hear nails scratch at our insides
Reminding us we are still in our box of fear trying
To get out we sometimes look in the mirror neatly

Placed right in front of our face, but we are only eyeing
Our small blemishes not really looking eye to eye with
Ourselves. So we live this way while squirming in our
Very clothes, not sure what it is we have buried and for

How long. I have opened my box of fear and let my
Ghost free, even though he still asks to dance with me.

# Frame 400: I Planted

Pine trees all summer. Three of them I planted four
Years ago. Both are eight feet tall. Nights the fog
Decides to leave my hill, the stars look down on me.
Ten thousand stares for one man. I often stand in front

Of one pine tree being admired. I fit my shadow within
Its borders. I start to stare as the wind blows my shirt
And what hair I have left. In that tree's shadow I realize
The absence of color. Like the night sky I am black.

I keep staring and the shadow seems to transcend. I move
With the shadow. Part of me begins to float away, then
Thought brings me back. Plato. Fire. Walls. Shadows.
We could be illusion and our thoughts, just ghosts, casting

Reality on the inside walls of our brains. I suspect spirit exists
In these shadows, where all remains faceless, not part of fear.

# Divine Dialogue

A friend told me to take a walk with Jesus, but I said I didn't know how.
So she advised, "Just pretend He is there, like when you were a child,
Make Him an imaginary friend, talk to Him." And so I did. With my flannel
Shirt, faded jeans and hiking boots I strolled by rhododendron, with their

Trumpet-shaped flowers rising out of the forests of West Virginia. I continued Along mountain trout streams, painted by shining sunlight, as if silver rippled Under the water and over the rocks. As a man I fish these waters looking now for Answers I never asked as a boy. As the wind picks up, I witness turkeys,

Deer, Rabbits and squirrels – all of which I hunted in a more hungry season. But Nowadays I am starved for conversation and meaning. So I chat with Jesus. For hours, imagined or real, I have my conversation with Him confessing I am Lost. That I need better bullets to fight evil than I have loaded in my gun.

As I start to leave this wilderness I feel something grab my hand, startling me at First, but then I turn around seeing I can travel fearlessly back Home.

Bill Garten

# Too Cold To Bark

My dogs hope for the garage which is not heated
But warmer than outside where the wind and bitter cold
Has haunted their short hair all winter they rush
In every time I come home and pop open the garage

Door too cold to bark at me or anything else they
Sleep most of the night and dread me coming in the early
Morning to let them out and out they go, going quickly
And yearning to come back in they run back to their cages

Which any other time would be restraining and confining
But need beats luxury and I don't know if they think about
The sun they drank up all summer and how the nuisance
Of biting flies would be better than this cold, this winter

Where sometimes they do bark on warmer days, calling for heat
And exercising their lungs, reminding themselves of seasons.

# Acting Out

Or at least this is what my therapist calls it. For years I visit my brain
Like it's a movie theatre and my life is the feature film filled with all
That haunts me. So I want in the middle of the night. I walk and go by
My dad's old Victorian house which is for sale. I sit on the curb and write

A poem on a scrap piece of paper. The broken brick street has street lamps
Now and I move on stopping down the street at her house to slip the poem
Under her doormat. She is sleeping. I am pretty sure. I don't know if she will
Throw away the poem or read it. I don't know her anymore. So I stop in

A bar. Get drunk. Try to pick up some woman. I get rejected even though I
Think she is an easy mark. So I go and pay for it. Find a strip bar. End
up in a Hot tub looking for a kiss and a hug. But I scare them easily.
Being too needy.
And the owner throws me out for being too aggressive. Breaking unwritten

Rules. But he tells me to come back when I am more sober. When I
can Behave. That he has other girls, more experienced, who can help.

Bill Garten

# In This Bathtub

In this grave of water I pull my scrotum's skin over my penis
Covering him up, he looks like a turtle with its head sticking
Out, but this turtle is going no where. He is stuck under this
Soft flesh shell here in my father's old Victorian home with its

Bear claw bathtub. I think about how we deal with things like
Expectations and somewhere in the bell curve of standards
There is this acceptance of one's self and the shadows we cast
With our thoughts our bodies can be obstructed from view

With this soapy water blurring vision, the picture of myself
With clothes and without clothes can still hide, still afraid to come
Out I am comfortable in my own skin until outside interference,
Life itself, forces me to deal with death - a card game I don't want

To play. These turtle thoughts can be dark and also blinding as if they
Are bright light. The light at the end of the tunnel. Peeking head on.

# Memory Train

We board it every day some moment or another constantly going
Somewhere we have been before it is addictive to live in the past,
Some kind of natural pharmaceutical escape we possess in our brains
Which have become our chemical synaptic cesspool and today while

Driving to go snow skiing I hear an old song on the radio from that
Time where we flocked to the watering holes of disco, where we chased
Those long tan mannequin legs with meaningless abandon I licked
olive
Nipples right off tender young breasts under black light seduction

It was the days of  Dionysian dancing on top of color lighted glass
Floors and kisses that lasted so long they left you coming up for air.
I thought the longer the kiss the more breathless the better, like a good
Run or swim I wanted to gasp from passion and exhausted from want

Memory is triggered today, like a migraine it is painful riding on this
Train, locked in my seat with the landscape of me flying by.

# Frames Revisited

I don't remember falling asleep
But I do remember thinking of you
Right before I did and my thoughts
Sprouted like so many buds on a tree

In early Spring. This morning the sun
Came to my eyes and I could hear
My body whistle as I inhaled through
My tea pot nose I sounded like a wind

Or a tree frog chirping pitch. This sinus
Condition this heart condition this
Condition that is out of condition
Thinking green thoughts that turn brown

With emotion. That fall like so many leaves. Eyes fall on this
White ground. This sheet. Crap thoughts. Clean paper.

# On The Way

To see your father you wiped the windshield with your hand
Complaining of the rain that you couldn't see ahead to spot
Your dad's eighteen wheeler. I gave you my blue bandana and
You worked at the foggy glass, finally seeing your smile beamed.

You were taking him a candy cane for Christmas that we both
Painted for him but I told you not to tell him I helped and it
Was for him like the time you would spend together. On the way
You and I talked about all that you and on the way

Back your mother used the same blue bandana to blow her nose
To wipe her face and make up smudged by her tears she complained
About the rain and her arthritis and how divorce dictates more pain
Than marriage did at times and how she had the small reassurance

That this whole visitation thing was protocol and fair and that it
Was the price she had to pay - that you'd be back by the weekend.

Bill Garten

# Thoughts In A Turks and Caicos Bar

For Pete's Corner dedicated to Peter Breck Holden 1946-2003

I never knew Pete or anyone who did know him. The bartender
Knew of him and only that his name and life dates are engraved
In this wooden bar here where he usually sat and now his little
Death marker, like a tombstone, is permanent for now a lot

Like me looking around watching the cleavage of women
In their bikinis and how the curves and shadows of their
Breasts are like Venus flytraps enticing my eager hungry eyes
As one more time I venture out on the tightrope of love, working

Another relationship without a net and with the quickness of a lizard
I can become so still only so cognizant that I get caught up
With what can be captured and as a man I can change as many colors
Or outfits to finally camouflage, trick and pretend to be that someone

I am not just so I can eat and survive, finally chomping down I rub
My unshaven chin realizing it is rough as wood in need of sanding.

# It Was The Sixties

Other than the sun dawning upon me this AM I see how I fell
In love with you at the carnival that hot August day when it came
To town with its elephants and rides and when I was trying so
Hard to win your love I shot those cheap BB guns at those

Metal ducks, tigers, and bears being pulled along the horizontal
Landscape under a tent by some invisible pulley mechanism
And when I won I won this big stuffed animal that you carried
Around all day and slept with that night and I was proud

To call you mine that somehow with you wearing my letter
Sweater, my school ring, and having you by my side at every
Dance and every game the world knew you belonged to me
This beautiful model that was taught and learned and the way

We set up house and started taking shots at each other daily
As you drove around in your sports car with diamonds and fur.

# At 2AM I Wake Up

Lately I have been feeling captured by my own skin
Confined by life so for a distraction I go on a trip
Fly away somewhere

Making my world bigger and I get drunk
To forget about it all
For just a day

But I still end up back
Where I was
Am

And that is limited by a world
That has the same headlines and
Rules and trapped here this way

By what we call life reality this dimension
I grow angry because it really is not enough.

# Wardrobe Change

I've backed into this figured it out
There is no way I can wear all the clothes
I have to wear by the time I can wear
Them they will not be worn out

Like my body, mind, spirit, soul, heart
Self I have overbought the on sale part
Of life and not being prudent more utilitarian
In my ways I have wasted money wasted

Efforts wasted waste this is not really sinful
Or even punishable by death or material but it is
Some sort of material cotton, silk, polyester
Worsted wool that is not worse off because

It won't be worn out like the days I lived
Exhausted with words, with the quick stitching of me.

Bill Garten

# Orange Enlightened Faces or The Candle Within

I am sure the monks in Nepal or Tibet are
Chopping wood and carrying water
After chores they are meditating

Trying to achieve oneness.

Here in West Virginia I am burning trash,
Feeding and watering animals.
I chopped wood in a hot September sun
But I have enough for any winter

So my wood chopping is done.

After my tasks are mentally marked off I have this feeling
Of completeness but instead of meditating I line up the
Rejected Halloween pumpkins from my garden on a far

Away wall and while drinking a six pack of beer on my porch I
Shoot at the imagined Jack o' lantern smiles that never got carved.

# On A Late February Morning

The wood thrush
Brown as any fallen leaf
        As any winter branch
        As any river stone


Calls for a potential
Mate
At dawn outside
My bedroom window

But no mate
Shows
Her face
On my pillow

My feathered
Heart sings.

Bill Garten

# My Head Was Full Of You

For four years, but now I am trying to empty
You out, like something gone bad in the refrigerator

You smell and everything else is tasting bad
Because of you and everything else is of you

It is hard to swallow to believe we ate and drank over
Candlelight while engulfed in ocean views and horizons

Of hope in each other and our eyes stared into
The invitation of flames and sunsets and moon

Walks and we were mesmerized by their warmth
The dance the very way the flickering in each of us

Twirled with our emotions and the ballerina in our
Hearts leaped but now the shore licks the shore

The flame licks the air and my shadow is cast out
Grabbing moments, pawing at this empty dark.

# Cayman Island Realization

Last night
I had this dream

Your beautiful face
Was a gigantic valley

Under this vast
Baby blue sky

As the clouds blew
Through your hair

As you smiled at me
I was suspended on a tall cliff

And then I dove into the green
Welcoming waters of your eyes

Swimming in you forever
There was no more pain.

Bill Garten

# Flakes Of Snow

Float down reminding me of the aspirin I take each morning
For my heart. There are oceans of white lava clouds reflected

In the dark water of my pond, which I have stocked with bass,
Blue gill, catfish and Koi. Earlier I caught and released some

Of each, the Koi finally realizing worms were not their delicacy,
So they decide to wait for my hand thrown pellets. Later after

Sunset I punch the dark throwing my fists in anger like a boxer
Practicing or shadow boxing. Here in the light of dusk my gold

Wedding ring catches my eye like shiny fish fins pretty as any
Necklace on any young neck. The fish randomly French kiss

Searching the water's surface but quickly dart, fade with this cold
Weather and in December below the ice they will be immune

To agony like my memories of you I will use wine to freeze
My own waters while I hibernate in my house in the unfed dark.

# Nature's Recall

The blue jay came at dawn quickly
I saw it as I dressed for work
The day my father died
I saw one outside our church's window

Come evening I planted three river hastas
Where the blue jay left a single feather
And after picking it up I dug a hole
Deep enough to plant a Gingko tree.

It was the third Gingko I have planted.
I was the last of three sons. For luck
I have done this at every residence.
Three hastas and three Gingko trees.

I see the same April moon as it was ten years ago
When my father died. There are white jet streams
In the night sky – brief lifelines. Health, like
A loosely put on hat, blows away.

Bill Garten

# You Know

Those bubble wrap things
We get in the mail to protect precious
Other things from breaking

Slipping around I play
With this packaging popping trapped
Air over and over again

Until I start stressing you out
With my firecracker relief
I get rid of my tension

Driving you to cook dinner
In the next room until I come
To you with my tongue, my taste

Buds now bubble wrap and you turn
Hungrily toward me with your mouth

# Frame 302

I met an Indian. She would prance
Like midnight water over flat rocks

By the river by my cabin
Her hair was black

Rippling over the white cloud
Pillow pulse of my bed

Her skin tasted like caviar
And her throat swelled with laughter

As the flesh at the top of her breasts
Jiggled with youth

Her teeth, white pebbles, moved under
The currents of my breath

Where I snatched the minnow,
The language of her tongue.

# Frame 303

Clipping my toenails in the sun as it shines through the Venetian blinds
I see trees shedding their leaves for their winter sleep. Fading, our love
Drifts through the branches scattering shafts of light on the water. I
Visit the water after our separation for my own healing, making bark ships

Like I did as a child. My navy. Fog floats in over the meadow and ghosts
Seem to dance where the tall grass meets the woods. Deer rest there at night
Like the witch, who is rumored to occupy the woods. There is a beaver who
Has built a dam to the East and I launch my little boats not wanting
to attack

Anyone anymore. As children, you and I played in our innocence because
We liked each other and your phone calls followed me to boot camp and
Around the world. Your letters - written life lines. What touched us then
Does not touch us now. Brown jets of hair surround your eyes in my

Wallet picture of you. You told me you could love a man even though his
Hands had embraced the rhythm of guns. At the time you didn't know
You were lying. Like the moth I have found streams of light unaware
Of the black wick they come from. Black breath death.

# Frame 304

With a contract
Renewed on pain

I move away from you
Damaged

Damage
It is what

We try to replace
With the parts

From other people
As we go along.

Small wonder
This renewal

This glue that goes beyond
The kiss of repair.

# The One Piece

Of rotten banana
Out my

Jeep window
Driving to work

This morning
May be the last scrap of food

For a starving opossum
Or wild dog willing to rush

West Virginia
Route 10

Curving and swerving
Black asphalt snake road

Heavy coal trucks
Rolling tires

# You Sat

Down as if you had
Something to say

But silent you watch the snow
Bits of clouds defining winter

Flakes of God's dandruff you call them
You've never seen snow since you always

Lived in Florida all these years and you
Watch me feed the birds, flecks of seed

On the deck, small offerings,
This new place without your mother

Where you seem to watch me and all
Around me everywhere I am you follow

Now outside
And in you she works your memory

Bill Garten

# There Are Those Nights Even Now

That I still miss you. I don't really truly know why.
Between the loss of you and the anger I have toward

You I still can't hate you. Though I have tried. And I wish
For days where I will be so busy that I don't think of you.

You were like my cigarette habit. So bad for me.
I would pull on the levers of never of that machine

Pack after pack addicted to you. I broke away only to want
You. Need you. And what I have given up and what I haven't

Taken on because of you is the composition of who I am now.
Not that it is pathetic. After all you didn't want me in the end

And that is perhaps the greatest pain. Maybe I tired to win you
And that was my insecurity. My mistake. And that made all

The difference. The only relief I get is on certain nights I can't
Recall your face. So as they say I got that going for me.

# Frame 305: On Our First Date

I bring you cut flowers. On a whim I pick them up at the grocery store.
You can't find a vase. I suggest the tennis can by the door. One week
Later the flowers are still alive. You tell me that the secret is to empty
Out the icky water daily. On the way up the Ohio River, we talk about

The bends and curves and the way the road follows the river. The lights
On the various bridges reflect and hang like colored icicles in the black
Waters. You tell me you love the chemical plants and the telephone
Poles and progress. The wires endlessly stretching along the road

Showing you the world is trying to communicate. We eat at the Well's Inn
In Sistersville. I have lobster. Its mermaid tail curves up, anxious to be
Devoured. Your crab legs point at the other guests. We are so involved
We do not notice them. Or their town. Here they drill for oil. Refine it.

On the way back we travel no on the West Virginia side of the river but
The Ohio side. Little did we know then we would end up in Ohio
Twenty two years later. That night I saw a falling star. I hurriedly told
You but you missed it. You asked me back then if I made a wish and

I did. Growing nervous I changed the subject. I started talking about
Hummingbirds. How their long beaks probe and draw pollen from flowers.

# Frame 306

It seems when I blink my eyes see me
Digesting this darkness.

Being a breath
From being further away

From myself
You hug me like a man would but you

Are a woman. This half hug is what
I am left with and as your lips touch

My unshaven cheek I look beyond you
As you pat my back there is nothing

You can say to bring back what I feel
I am abandoned

Like a hive
Where the queen is dead.

# Frame 307

My wife is a morning person. If I had longer teeth
I would roam the night hunting other animals.

Noise bothers me as I get up. Overhead lights bother me
Too. My wife likes the radio alarm wake up world

And hair dryers. I am bald and like birds waking me up.
I can't sing but my wife does in the shower. If I hum

The dogs would start to whine. Today I did a little dance
Right before I put on my pants. I let out a whistle

On my way to pick up the newspaper. I am scared to say
That I might be as happy as I can be happy but I wouldn't

Want to jeopardize anything. I never really relied on the
Word happy much. Too many smiley faces floating around

For the likes of me. But at night when I see the alarm clock
With its lighted time and I look at her I see dark traces redefined.

# Frame 308: Ill Prepared

Repairing, you make up your face.
This morning this is pop art to me.

You dab at the loss.
Last night's absence of me drove

You to my door. Usually I don't come
In until dawn, but you called and I fix

Breakfast. You explain how you burnt
Dinner and how your husband got mad

And this morning as you develop this new portrait
Of yourself, the only criteria is when you are good enough

You leave me and go back out to the world where
You don't want anyone to know about your

Bruises and other signs of abuse. You come to me
So I can eat your mistakes, the part of you overdone.

# Fighting Dreams

It was and still is what I know when I tuck myself into sleep
I have to pull the cover or sheet or blanket over my right
Shoulder to make sure I am tucked in all the way and I know
My mother must have done this when I was a baby making

Sure I had this cover over all my body except for my head
No need to worry about suffocation or anything dangerous
As she sat on the edge of my bed in the hospital she made sure
One more time to tuck me in and let me know comfort

And I know I rubbed my feet together before I went to sleep
As a baby as I do now trying to reassure myself in some prenatal
Way that the pictures they showed us this evening of me
And my heart, looking like a piece of marbled meat,  are not as bad

As the surgeons believe and that days from now they will do their
Job weaving me new rivers of life, helping my heart sing again.

Bill Garten

# What Did It For Me

The first time was after my heart catheterization in 1996 and how
In a hurry you did not let me know about the weather as you drove
Me home from the hospital you did not make any arrangements
Other than maybe secretly in your head for my funeral, but when

We got there at the bottom of our WV hill you and I knew your Benz
Would not make it up the mile steep incline and when I asked you
Why you didn't bring the jeep, you said you weren't thinking (of me )
And you had a business conference call and you asked if I could

Make it on my own and I said if I fell it could open up the slice
In my leg only hours old enough to be discharged and if it burst
I could bleed out in thirty minutes, but as usual you did not hear
And you took off walking ahead abandoning me in my limping

March, like Sisyphus, I climbed upwards while the heavy snow fell
Around my feet testing for ice and a heart tightening with the cold.

# It's Not All About You or
# What Also Did It For Me

Was years later when we reunited and I was processing all your old
Checks at tax time I discover all these names of people I have never
Heard of and when I asked you don't know or recall or whatever
It was you had no memory you said and it was only later in therapy

With our daughter when she told me and the therapist that you used
To leave her with total strangers around the park or in some unknown
Neighborhood while you got your exercise routine in you left our
Daughter who was four years old at the time with complete strangers

And you would pay them for their time and all this so you could be fit
And look prettier than you think you ever can be and when I asked
you
About the price our daughter paid you in your insensitive manner
Said she was too young to know or remember or recall or whatever

It was all about you and no matter you had to get rid of your business
Stress no matter what it cost you had to cope regardless the price.

# Camouflage

It's not just for chameleons and fawn, you do it quite well
With your cosmetics and personality, but unlike a reptile or
Animal you advertise not trying to hide at all but instead you
Beg for me, your bug buddy to swim toward your bulb of

Beauty where I become your moving mirror and validate you
Over and over again with my adoration and my hope of
Just getting the chance to be close to you, but this is my own
Illusion that I could actually break into your prison where I

Could be your inmate of intimacy, where I could actually
Strip away your sheets and see the bareness you have learned
So well to cover, but instead I entertain myself and you
Daily, until I don't even know how or what I am hiding in

And it is really me who has camouflaged myself so
You won't really see the real me so I can get more near.

# Frame 309: Credit

There's plenty of it, like air
The banks are glad

To lend it, like a corner drug dealer
They hand it out getting

Us hooked. For someone
Who makes their living

With a pen I think tomorrow I will find
Another one and make chopsticks.

When the collectors call they take back
My belongings, the very collateral is the damage

I gave them and after they come to pick it
Up, they remind me when

The horse dies, they own the saddle,
A glue factory.

Bill Garten

# What Do I Do With This

Sadness? Serve it for breakfast over easy
Or wrap it up and send it to you
Via UPS? Brown or decorative paper?

It really weighs more than we can
Measure, but its heaviness has
Not slowed me down per se

No one would notice unless they
Physically stopped me, grabbed
Me and looked straight into my

Eyes and asked what is wrong?
And at first I would say I don't
Really know and toss them off

As if they were a piece of lint
That is not welcome during dress up.
But as I stop, not avoiding myself

I hear sadness calling me, begging
Me to step away from life
From the illusions we have built

Here. Illusions that just keep
Us busy, and occupied and so
Distracted. There will always

# What Do I Do With This (continued)

Be something to take our mind
Off what it should really be on.
There will always be the focusing

On the unfocused. So I hear it.
Its siren keeps begging me.
And tired I give in, begin to feed it

As if it were some stray cat.
And it needs to be fed but
Not taken care of.

It has learned how to do that on its
Own. It shows up hungry,
At my door periodically

Asking me to come explore the night
As it scurries toward
That darkness where it hides.

Bill Garten

# It Is Overcast Sunday

And I walk over my two suburban acres
Cleaning up sticks and larger tree limbs
Cast from last night's stormy winds
I can see the large pond that borders

My property, the pond that I stocked
Eight years ago with numerous bass,
Blue gill, catfish and a dozen Koi -
That the pond is starting its freeze.

I watch my two cats eat on my back porch
As I snip off the tricolored yarn I used
To hold up my tomato plants earlier this
Summer against the porch's cedar railings

With scissors in hand I look at these dry dead
Stalks, brittle to the touch. I imagine as I drop
Some bits of yarn, lazily leaving a little behind,
That a bird or two will use it for nest

Building next Spring and that I will be
Here to not necessarily see the birds
Snatch it up, but lucky enough to see the pond
Thaw. The boy in me anxious once again to see the

Brilliant golden Koi right under the water
And the man in me still wanting to feel the surprise
Of the tug on the line. Startled again that
I can catch something struggling, so wet

And squirmy
Other than these swimless thoughts.

# Acting Out

There is a buffet of women out there
I have found them as I have moved toward
The trash can of death.

In these motels and back rooms there are
Lessons on how we should turn to art,
And the nature of being quiet and really

Taking care of our elderly but these are
Goals on the way toward civilization
As the blood from our brains flows toward

Our groins and we engage like insects more
Than humans. It is a strange comfort, this
Closeness that I pay for. It leaves me

So empty of one thing and so full
Of another.

# Pills

I swore somewhere in my late teens
That if I ever had to take pills to stay
Alive I would just soon die

Here in midlife I approach fifty five
Like it was some mandatory speed limit
For staying alive

And I am with two pills for my stomach,
Two for my heart, two for allergies I picked
Up crossing fifty and an aspirin for good

Measure I do them every morning and night
Putting up the good fight.

# My Wife Has Sleep Disorders

So when I sleep with her so do I
Not getting enough sleep but she
Sleeps through these rare shared nights

She tremors and kicks like someone
Was holding her down but it is
Not me I am up reading so I can

Fall back asleep or find a good couch
In our home there is plenty of room
To escape from one another with

Our one daughter gone off to college
No one really knows
There is anything wrong.

Bill Garten

# Playing God With The Animals Again
# Or One Less Vet Bill This Year

While petting him I could not help but notice
It is pink, like the bubble gum liquid
Amoxicillin I gave my infant daughter
To get rid of her ear aches while growing up

When we slipped the needle in his forearm
He was suffering. Convinced, this is why we did it.
He trustingly looked at us like all the other
Times as if we were going to help whether

It be the chemo going in or drawing blood out
To see how far the cancer was chasing him hungry
As he used to be for the rabbit or the squirrel
The cancer as the Zen Master would say

Is alive and it wants to live and why we try
And kill cancer is out of self defense one of
Us has to make it and of course we want it to
Be us, but Chance did not have a chance

In the end we told ourselves we were doing
Him a favor and there wasn't anything else
Left to do and to this day as I am hauling
His dog house to the curb so the garbage men

# Playing God With The Animals Again
# Or One Less Vet Bill This Year (continued)

Can take it away on Thursday or as I am taking out
The extra cage we had for him in the garage
I will wonder if I should have waited or given
Him more time, another few days to see if

He would have turned, if only for a few more
Days. As it is with his extra cage gone there
Is more room in the garage for the mountain
Bikes and we will gripe less about the tight

Fit for the fourth car and how we won't bump
Our knees so easily moving about navigating in
The space we have left. Time and space.
Energy in that space. Rearranging for the

Convenience of our lives we adjust as if
Our belts are too tight after dinner or
The lighting is not just right so we turn on
A dime going about our business in our avoidance

Until it turns on us, death with its buffet of diseases
Waiting to grab us for a quick game of poker
Some lazy afternoon when we stop caring, He smiles
And ignorantly we play with our winning hope

Trusting as a dog on a metal slab in some back room
Drawing one last breath like it was a needed card.

# Chance

They take you down to a back room
Sort of hidden down the stairs shortly
After you make the decision, the one
We rarely or bravely make for ourselves

And then they tell you it is the right
Thing and you could spend more
Money and you could get one
Or two more rallies at best

But there is no guarantee even
That would happen so since you
Have already spent thousands, been advised
Not to throw more at it they reassure

You while they slip the needle in
That within twenty seconds there
Is this guaranteed sweet sleep
Something we all fear yet still run to

But so adequately provide for
Those who some of us think are lesser
Than ourselves. And so he slips away
With a breath - as you do out a provided

Back door where you can exit too
And you don't have to explain to anyone
If the zero degree weather hitting
Your face brings that tear or if

It was something you think you
Should have done or shouldn't have
But regardless it is done and it is
More than we do for ourselves - humans.

# Not A Poem, But An Uncut Thought For Someone Who Wrote Me An E-Mail

For years he walked around like this
Greeted by so called friends and liked by most in town
And what emotional holes he had inside couldn't be seen,
Not like the physical pain we witness when someone

Tells us or when we see it on faces in hospitals -
No, not this kind of pain. One learns to hide early
After feeling this kind of pain. So he, like others
Gladly placed on the tasks masks and went about doing

Errands and duities and keeping busy with this and that -
So many distractions that he, like others forgot
About the pain and the feeling of abandonment and
Not wanting to share too much beyond the easy he

Found the big compromise in avoiding it and there
Was always the card game on Tuesday night or
The golf game on Saturday or whatever event
Could make him and others like him forget and

So life became this living rolling freeze frame and it
Played while being stuck and this is how he and others
Ran their lives running from the pain and afraid to
Love and feel alive and so this edited irony

With its delightful trips and meals and clothes and
Art itself helped him and others like him dodge
The stopping of their own heart by really loving and
Daring to give themselves to someone else -

# Not A Poem, But An Uncut Thought
# For Someone Who Wrote Me An E-Mail
# (continued)

By being emotionally available as an option
That would be too hard and too difficult and too scary
Much like inviting that old pain to dinner and
Forgiving it for the damage it caused so long ago

Serving it your best gourmet meal and pouring it
Some fine wine and getting it drunk
After some good conversation and then
Not knowing whether to seduce it or cuss it out

For what it did so long ago,
But all that would be such a socially
Unacceptable risk about why it happened
In the first place or how it could get back

To where it was before the painful part
And if it could only just not be there not leading to
This all said and done, he woke and worked
Like so many others and went about his business

Not trying to get in the way and going with the flow
Until he was dead like so many others - life so unlived.

# It's The Simple Pleasures

Like walking the dog and feeding the birds
In winter jerking off in a separate bedroom
On nights I tell her she was snoring and
Keeping me up – not really – I do that

Myself most of the time in the morning after
I shower spotting my Swank brush that I know
Must be forty years old since my mother gave
It to me my first year in prep school in Asheville

North Carolina and this brush is in such good
Shape for being forty so unlike me. The reason
The brush has lasted so long is I went bald at
Twenty-two so the brush didn't have a hard

Career like I have – so many jobs that didn't work
Outright, like so many nights sleeping with my wife.

# Love Poem For Anne

Going to the pharmacy for my heart pill
I realize that there is so little time in my life
I wake up and eat my oatmeal and decide
To send you my books, not to sleep with my wife

Then onto the dry cleaners and the office
And perhaps a swim in the afternoon of course
The Board meeting tonight which will be way too
Long, from 6:30 - 11:30PM, not ending very soon

And tomorrow I will start pretty much stuck the same
Way like a scratched record and the branch at night
That rubs up against the window trying to get in
This repeated thinking of you and today my father

How he told me after working in the yard he scraped his head
On a branch, the "flinch factor" not there, no warning, no hair.

# Confessing To My New Girl About A Love Gone By Or Why As A Man I Say No To Sex Like Women Can

She called from Colorado to fight some more
Our endless symbiotic emotional little tug of war
She tells me I should have made love to her
When she asked the week before she married

But I was selfless and made a judgement call
More for her and her hubby to be than me
But she still blames me for not coming through
After thirty five years you'd think giving up

Would be better than living up to the lie
We've made true - she with her films and money
And me in my dark place filled with honey
Flames from a fire that now only burns for me

So like the child's balloon not by surprise but
Deliberately I let go looking up briefly not caring
If it makes it to where it can't be seen
Or bursts on its way to something new

This is what we do when we are ready
To move from one part of our life to the next
And perhaps someone was already pulling me
In another direction where there are golden

Meadows and flowers and a balmy wind
Not tangled by branches and narrow passages.

# Frame 5000: Blue Jays

Blue Jays eat out of the cat bowl
Rollins leaves food every morning on the cedar deck
The cats are too lazy, too relaxed in the afternoon sun
To hunt the Jays

Rollins picks a large tomato that broke the very vine
That supported its growth
The praying mantis on the bent stem
Looks more like a brown walking stick

As it is stretched out in meditation
Not praying at all
The dogs do not bark
The bird feeders are full

But the Jays do not like the seed and suet buffet
They fly, sweep in and prefer Meow Mix
Meow Mix meddled by the thieving raccoons
Waking Rollins at three in the morning

As he sleeps on the blue couch in the sun room
A little upset as usual
The cats, the dogs, the Jays are all dreaming
Now

But not Rollins, who watches the mother raccoon fight with her children
Over the deep dish cat food bowl. Meow Mix. Meow Mix.
He notes that a spider has built a web by the porch light
Catching moth meals while another praying mantis or perhaps

The same one chows down on something with only its wings
remaining.
His back hurts where wings would be
But Rollins has no wings.
These pains are only symptoms.

# Frame 5001:  Tithing

Rollins empties his trash. Weekly he does this. Each time feeling a little more
Accomplished.
Satisfied that he is getting rid of the stuff in his life.
There is no use for this or that so it becomes trash. The valued things, like old
Shirts, toasters, extra staplers make their way into bags for donations.

Salvation Army, Goodwill, church gatherers for disabled veterans. Even at church
The minister preached this week about stuff. How much stuff? What kind of stuff?
So Presbyterian sermon for a moment meets East. Zen warrior of trash
Rollins is getting Rid of Stuff. Emptying out.Trying to get to nothing
but a cot, a basin, a book and perhaps

One crucifix on the wall. Unable to sleep Rollins thinks about her.
The conversation.
When she briefly mentioned how she emptied the Sunday trash from the kitchen
While her father was hauling two suitcases into their station wagon.
Leaving. Leaving
Her mother. Her family. Rollins imagines her painted there. All of seventeen in a garage

Rollins had traveled through on the way to ping pong games, endless dinners with
Endless conversations. Plato and Socrates would have been happy to be drooling above
Those philosophical plates. The garage that led to the kitchen that led to the hall that led
To the den where adolescent eyes were big, where adolescent arms and legs could

# Frame 5001: Tithing (continued)

Not get enough petting passion. Rollins never made love to her.
He had a naive Ingredient that was taught him. Don't take away
something you can not return. Don't pick A flower you do not intend
to water. Forever. So he didn't. And now he tries to imagine Her face.
Her tears as her father emptied those two cases into the trunk. What
emptying

In that moment took place? What parts of stuff got taken away and
what would not return? Rollins moves about the room. He looks for
things to throw away. His mind keeps revolving about the trash. When
he is gone. Dead. Someone will empty out what Rollins could not. His
clothes, his unused gun. His poems, head memories that occupy his

Brain like dishes in a cabinet. Stuff unbroken. Hopefully someone will
use them. Dine on their chips and cracks. Philosophically admire what
pattern or color they still hold. Perhaps there will be recalled joyous
laughter. That laughter of an adolescent girl who Rollins remembers as
being happy, her laughter reassuring her she was happy.

And actually aware she was enjoying it. She could be happy and laugh.
Not the kind of laugh her sister nervously produced as the two of them
bathed their dying mother. It was a laugh that emptied fear. The fear
didn't have a shape or name at the time. It took years for the fear to be
called properly what it should be called, a fear that fears laughter.

# Frame 5002: Rollins On The Back Porch

The September sun feels warm like the red wine
In his throat. The raccoons will ravish the scraps

Of salmon the cats didn't finish. Rollins looks
Through the trees and sees several leaves skating

On top of the pond. Earlier he cut the grass, trimmed
A hedge, played toss with a tennis ball with his two dogs.

It isn't death he is afraid of like he had thought
All these years. He is really afraid of being nurtured.

After all the only time he had ever been nurtured
Was when he had a near death experience.

Waking in his father's arms at five after being in a coma
For three days. Crying in a black nurse's bosom

After an operation and a motorcycle accident.
Or the time a lady came in his hospital room

And talked to him about God and angels only to find
Later she did not work at the hospital in any capacity.

He is tired of having to almost die
Just to get the comfort he needs while living

So he isn't afraid of death at all
He is afraid he has to almost die to find

The degree of love he yearns for while alive.
Like the fire in the propane grill

# Frame 5002: Rollins On The Back Porch

It has to reach a certain degree to be effective
To cook the fish, to get it done.

Rollins realizes he doesn't have to die to get love.
To get it done. The wine all of a sudden tastes a little better.

The wind feels easier and the pain, or whatever
It is that woke him the night before is lighter.

# Frame 5003:  Many Early Mornings

Rollins wakes disturbed by dreams
He sits in the sun room with all its artwork,
Plants and the steady aquarium noise

He gazes out the windows to witness
Fog rising like ghosts from the fish pond
These spirits are not lost

They seem to have direction
And too quickly they are gone
Unlike Rollins bothered by these

Days, these restless moments where
Reality is not quite right in his mind
Thoughts come and go of people

Moving in and out of lives
These emotions, silent ethereal passages
Haunt his heart

He feels it filling up its chambers
Pumping and emptying out
Gurgling like it is hungry

Bill Garten

# Frame 5004:  Coincidence or Question Mark

Wovoka, a Paiute Indian holy man in Nevada taught the
Native American Indians the Ghost Dance religion
Where tribes would bring back their dead ancestors, the
Buffalo, wisdom and peace. The White man thought

This peaceful loud Ghost Dance was a war dance so the Indians
Were slaughtered.
Perception. It is a problem. Hume addresses this.
Plato does. So many philosophers and Rollins have

Noticed there are shadows on the wall, but they do not
Always represent the things casting the shadows.
And the light, where is it other than in the sun, the bulb,
The fire?

In a cave when there is no light the eyes can't dilate
And you can experience, according to those who can see:
Blindness. So as a White man, Rollins gets curious about
What genetic structure in the White man makes him so

Vicious. So conquering. Is there some Viking gene or
Barbarian DNA floating around that makes us come
To quick conclusions justifying our slaughtering, attacking, and wiping out
Other species? And what about Wovoka? Where is his crucifix?

Why isn't every sock hop, disco, and dance studio hanging
A picture of Wovoka on the wall?
Rollins puts on some music. Starts dancing and singing
As he cleans up his apartment. Suddenly there is a huge banging

On the floor. The man in the apartment below is mad at the sudden noise.
His broomstick handle hits repeatedly his ceiling, which is Rollins' floor.

# Frame 5005: Heat, Reheat

Rollins heats clam chowder his wife made in the microwave thinking about a conversation
He would have if she were here. He gave her the recipe yesterday. She works long hours.
She does meal management this way. Rollins picks up his daughter at boarding school Where she does not board. The two arrive at a neat, organized clean house. Monday is maid
Day and Rollins has never met the maid in person. The maid keeps the house the way Rollins' mother used to keep house. He writes the checks, leaves
Them on the kitchen counter. The same counter that catches his bowl as he burns his Fingers reheating his soup. The only interfacing Rollins has had with the maid is when he
Made her a house key. When she first started. And the house always looks great on Mondays. It feels like home. Or the home Rollins used to have growing up.
And he is grown up now. Reading in the sun room and bothered by a male Cardinal trapped between the holly bushes and the window.
For some reason the bird is obsessed with himself in the window. Pecking it and fluttering Up against it. Leaving crap on the outside ledge, preoccupied with himself
Rollins every ten minutes goes over and scares him away. When dark falls the crazy Cardinal is gone. Perhaps the cardinal is drunk on berries. And so is Rollins. Crazy day,
Numbed by alcohol and more reading. Thirsty for knowing something other than what has already been, Rollins asks his daughter on a break how her day was - how school was
It was and there is a boy on the phone and so there is more reading and more drinking and Eventually Rollins goes to bed and brushes and flosses and looks in the mirror the way a
Cardinal looks into a window and the only difference is Rollins knows it Is a mirror and the reflection is Rollins, not a potential mate, not a shot at being engaged.

# Stolen

Sunday I was fishing and catching a few large mouth bass
When the cell vibrated, tugged at my belt the way a bite jerks a line
It was my wife
Her purse stolen at Walmart
Apparently by a black woman and black man
Running a scam
So to the rescue
In my jeep
When I got there, there she was guarding her car
They took everything
House keys, car keys, money, credit cards, driver's license
She felt violated
But the cop didn't as he took the report
His police dog barked in the back of his cruiser
At the air
No pot or coke or bad stuff here
Just yuppies making out a police report
During which the thieves ran up thousands on the cards
Even though I stopped them via cell
Driving to the rescue it wasn't quick enough
The damage done
We came home and got all nine locks replaced
Another $475. And there were more phone calls
To the credit reporting agencies, to the cops again
That the thieves were at a gas station and surely they had one of those
Cameras
We got the exact time and everything
But this is a possee of one
A detective working it when he can
So we went to bed less secure
To wake up to rain on Monday
And a flash flood
In the creek that feeds my fish pond

# Stolen (continued)

It rose to our deck
That I stripped two weeks ago to stain
But the rain
All summer it seems
Just like this last winter
We have lost the sun in Ohio and so much more
And now on the television they tell us two have drown
Downtown
The worst flood in a hundred years
And my favorite restaurant where I go and eat spinach salads and get
drunk
On red wine after my winter swim workouts
It's gone
Swept away
And with the Grand Piano I played "Moon River" on my fiftieth
birthday
With some blonde who liked plastic surgery and what it did for her
And what she did
For me.

# Playing Catch With Dad

A wooden three step foot
Ladder tall enough to make me
As big as you but it didn't

I was barely four
When you said
*Jump into my arms*

As you took a step
Back I can still recall
Your deep cigarette voice

As I fell
No blood, no bruises
Just shock that you weren't

There as you picked up
My crying body you whispered
*Never trust anyone, not even me*

# Growth

At the Doctor's office I sit on the table like a child on a swing
Swinging my legs back and forth just enough not to hit anything
I am nervous but distracted by the weed eater machine outside the
window
Cutting into green life on this sunny June summer day

The Doctor asks me how long has it been there and I say a week,
maybe ten
Days. She decides quickly we should cut it out and of course biopsy
the mass.
The shot in the testicle did not hurt as much as I thought. The
vasectomy years
Ago was worst and of course it was nothing even close to a good kick.

Waiting for the numb and the Doctor to return I think about coming
up on fifty
What I might do with the next twenty-five years if granted that many
I think of the cyst or growth or whatever and how it is trying to start
its seed
Trying perhaps to take me over. Stitches follow and instructions and
the wait

A week to find out if it is cancer, if it is alive and doing well, how
young it is
And if we should pull our swords out and yell the battle scream.

# Going To Sleep

My feet are hands
Rubbing together with worry

My legs
One long handle

As my brain flips
To one side

Then to the next
Then over again

This bald head
Tossing over easy

In this pillow pan
Hot with fever

Not yet done
In sleep

Eating dreams
Dead births

# 11/16/02

Remember the girl I told you about that I used to date in high school and she and I spent oodles of hours on her couch in her rich family's downstairs den listening to Santana and The Beatles kissing and hugging and petting but never making it doing it always falling short of making love the big deed and so we broke up because this little blonde wanted me to take her out and after I did she popped my cherry devirginated me in the back of my Pontiac LeMans Sport 350 on top of a hill under a clear night with all these stars and me looking up afterwards with all this guilt so in her wisdom she said let's do it again and we did and I didn't feel so guilty after the second time anyway this girl I told you about who I spent all this time kissing and never getting totally called me tonight from her private jet as she was zooming back from Paris on her way to New York and she said she had been thinking about me and how she misses me and how she just had an affair with this French guy and that she was going to tell her husband and he would probably tell their three boys and she didn't care anymore just like when after we broke up in high school cause the first boy she went out with after me for spite she did it with him and got pregnant and her mother who is dead now by the way made her get an abortion and then years later while she is married after having her third boy her dad brings a woman to Thanksgiving dinner and the woman happens to be the mother of the boy who got her pregnant in the first place years ago and nobody knew, not her dad, her husband or anyone and so she just smiled and was a nice hostess so anyhow this girl I used to date in high school calls me tonight from her private jet in route from Paris to New York and tells me she's been thinking about me and just as I am getting into the conversation my wife walks in with flowers, a fruit basket and an anniversary card for me for our sixteenth which I didn't forget but I just decided not to get her flowers or anything because this morning we agreed the money would be better spent on clothes for her and her new job so anyway I have to cut the conversation short because we have to hurry to our monthly bridge church group but first I have to go and retrieve my daughter from our den downstairs where she is on the couch with a high school boy.

# 11/16/02

There was this girl called Chocolate who my friends introduced me to for a blind date and she wore sunglasses the whole date even after it grew dark we were eating on this French Restaurant's patio and I asked her if she was ever going to take her glasses off and she said no and didn't and afterward I drove her home and we ended up making love on her diving board with the pool lights on and the next day I had all these little dimple indentations on my back from that sandy no skid stuff they put on diving boards and so years later I am in Myrtle Beach at a golf tournament and spending some time with a friend who is dying of lung cancer and I come in late after being at a strip joint and a massage parlor with him drinking and I see the little red light blinking on the phone and I get the message and it's from Chocolate who is crying on the other end of the phone because she caught her husband with their maid and he took off for Florida and left her and her two daughters and it is all my fault because I didn't want to date her and introduced her to her cheating husband on a blind date and she said she tried to be a good wife fixed him coffee every morning while he watched CNBC and gave him head right there as the futures went up and she thought everything was fine and dandy and how he got bent out of shape when she caught him and that he threatened her with her grandmother's fire poker and I thought about her step dad and how he had I say a hundred or more rifles laid out in his den like he was Ben Cartwright and his three sons and him were reliving the Ponderosa and I thought how it must have surprised my friend who I introduced Chocolate to for that blind date when he came back from Florida she was in her living room with a cowboy hat on and nothing else but one her step daddy's guns.

# 11/16/02

How can two kisses last forever?

I don't know. But they have. Like some magical ghost they swam into my spirit and swirl around in my body like some small wind like those little miniature tornados you see from time to time outside picking up a few leaves in a spinning top motion and then dying down but these two kisses are not dying down they are continuous in me like some whirlpool spirit tattooing its permanent impact inside me set in motion orbiting forever within me your breath your salvia locked in and engaged captured in this body in this cage a connection where the bars are skin and the roars of our love are heard beyond body beyond this world there are kisses little big bangs quenching the thirsts of zillions of mouths quenching the desires of zillions of tongues quenching the thirsts of the very spirit inside each of us grabbing the ultimate fullness of being touched and comforted we are caught by the lure of this hope, this honorable tease that leads to two kisses that will last forever.

# Old Route 8

Has everything. An art studio fronting as a Brothel. A health food store with carrot and wheat grass juice. A sushi bar with all types of people. The nursery where you can buy the best Black Austrian pines. Feed store where dog and cat food are cheap by the bulk. And of course there is the little Italian restaurant that has the best halibut with hot drawn butter and great wine and there is this woman you take there who makes you laugh and think and hope and after in the parking lot in the rain she gives you a handful of presents all of which mean something to you the CD from your favorite movie, a journal for you to write in, some healing vanilla incense with an incense burner and some face cream for your dry skin you get from swimming a mile everyday. As you talk in the car for hours the waiters and waitresses leave as they close up but you don't notice except for their occasional startling of you and her as you embrace and then you drop her off and she leaves and you drive home in the rain knowing she can break your heart with just the wrong glance of her eye.

# Versions of Pain

The physical punches I endured from boys bigger than me and my father taught me how to laugh at pain so as not to show I was weaker and that no one could hurt me I learned to laugh and with my bring it on attitude I created the walls I needed to emotionally survive most conflicts and storms that came my way I handled until this morning at 3 AM I wake up and think of you and how I will lose you to the market place and how I love you more than you love me and that makes it unrequited which has the word quit right in it so I do.

# Alex At Fifteen

So many things are measured in life and some of them are in years.
When we cry out of happiness no one asks someone to count how
many tears.
When we are afraid it doesn't have to be because of numerous fears
It can be one. There is no rhyme to my one fear I always had. It was
not living long

Enough to see you grow up. It sounds like measuring and it was,
but now my fear has Been wiped away, like so many foggy breathed
windows in childhood
It is clear to me it is not fear now, but happiness. My one prayer to see
You mature was granted me. Your birthday wishes were my wishes
blown over

Fifteen years, 120 candles for you and 645 candles for me. A unified
breath so
Anxious that it wished only for the one wish to come true. The wish to
see you
Blossom into a young woman. So I am fulfilled by God or whatever
cosmos let
Me be part of your creation and development. The very being of you.

There is no way one can measure the love I have for you in my heart.
When I was fifteen in prep school the leaves danced and laughed at
night in the dark
Outside my small window. In the morning the leaves were silent as the
Moon waited in the sky for the sun to bury its glow. I was afraid and
alone, but I knew

No one invented a love gauge to measure how much love I would and
could hold for you Alexandra. In my heart you are a buffet of song
that is sung by a thousand birds in the Endless dawn of my soul, you
are the light of my day. I wish you years and years
Of happiness, health and laughter, your same laughter that erased my
fear, my loneliness.

# Distractions

Rollins has plenty. The mile swim any week night. The 5K run in the neighborhood.
And the weekly bicycle ride down the tow path through Sand Run Park.
They help him run. Run away and into each guilt shit sandwich he tries
to eat. He has grown used to his pain that it is now so comfortable. More
comfortable than health.

What language is it? He thinks he used to speak it fluently. Youth is
so broken like
The birdfeeders left out all winter. He fixes them, but not himself. On
Saturdays mostly
He plays a silly round of golf in the morning and goes to therapy in
the afternoon. Trying To throw away his marriage he manages to knot
the twist tie around the garbage bag

And it is all tucked in there, but too heavy to lift. So he drags it to the curb.
Some dumb idea that it could work. And it did. Almost seventeen years.
What language is it? He thinks he knows how to say hello and ask
where the bathroom is.
Here comes another ping pong volley with who is right, who is wrong
in the brain blame

Great game on the scorecard, but no one knows how bad the shots
really were.
There are ugly and good shots in golf, in love relationships, but no one
cares as long as
You get it in the hole soon enough. Men have been preaching it for
years. Get it
In the hole. Her hole. Did you score? Every teenage locker room is
surrounded

By the curious question. And everyone wants to know. Did you get her?
And if you don't tell, it drives them crazy. Like the media not knowing
So they make up enough of a story until they shake out the salt of the
Matter. Did you make her sweat? Did you taste her salt? And so the garbage
Bag gets dragged, dragged

# Distractions

Out like a bad marriage. And you go to therapy on Saturdays and find out all
You did wrong and right. And Rollins goes out Satruday night. Dressed up, he tees up
His game and starts searching for a new hole. He flowers it with conversation.
He frosts it with romance. He thinks about all the shots it will take to get there.

So the volley starts. That is the language. Back and forth, back and forth we engage
In dialogue. We flirt with possibilities. Approach. Retreat. Struggle. Wrestle.
This is the language. Trying to love. It is constant. Always here. Ready to be sunk
Into. A ball in a hole. A penis in a vagina. Two tongues probing. No words.

Then you run. You swim. You bike. You play golf. You do a million things
Missing it all. But not Rollins, not anymore, he has no desire to brag or play.

# December 26, 2002

Sometimes I think I have to do something wrong in order to get my own attention to what is right.

I guess it is possible to fall in love with the wrong person. To blindly love someone without seeing how you are becoming their victim and perhaps they are becoming your victim as well.

The man of music met the man of faith and the man of music said, "I can't imagine a world without music. We would all go insane without it. We have lots of music in the world."

The man of faith agreed but also remarked "I can't imagine a world without prayer. Without it we would go insane. There is a world without prayer. Perhaps there is more music than prayer.

A third man overhearing the conversation said, "Perhaps music is prayer."

I guess there have been other times in my life that I have fallen in love or fallen for someone and not been able to love them. This is the strongest sadness for me. Not being able to find out if a certain person was really the one. I have always felt there is really only one.

# Black Hole

It's the place Rollins refers to when he loses things. Perhaps black holes
Can turn grey. Today he lost his sunglasses adding to his puzzle.
It could have been anything else: keys, watch, favorite ball cap
Heart medicine. He does this subconsciously to entertain himself
Secretly testing his brain to see if it can really remember which
Pocket, perhaps in the car, or on the back porch next to the wine

Where he read the book sent just yesterday from the author
Rollins loved a decade ago. He could have had a child with her
If she hadn't aborted it. But no one knows, she didn't know
Who the father really was. There were so many other candidates
A surprise to Rollins, but not to her. She wanted to be pregnant again
Because motherhood was her career, what she did best besides writing

Off the lost child like some bad debt she could not decide who to blame
And afterwards she left blood and pain in the wake of her maternal enema
Leaving Rollins a surprise of how much he could punish himself for
being
Just part of their crime of love and all the rewards it brought
Like the diamond ring thrown up against a wall in anger,
It settled like so many broken promises, word fossils forgotten.

But they aren't forgotten. Stolen from time, we develop our own history.
Each of us. Rollins has, you have, like some bad hand in cards we try
To get just a little more luck, some wrinkled hope there is a chance.
Tomorrow there will be a slight sore throat, a stuffy nose, perhaps
A muscle ache where there wasn't one before. Something Rollins has
To do. An errand. A new project. Something really worthwhile.

Staying busy has taught him he can learn to forget anything.
Something to distract him. Something beyond the urges
Of his flat bellied youth. Some lesser sought out pain.

# The Hygienist Comments

On me, my cotton button down shirt so stiff
Behind my tortoise shell frame glasses slightly

Scratched my fifty year old teeth a mix of white
And gold stones, little dominos crowded together

In the floor of my mouth in the roof of me
Hiding behind the very heavy starched collar

She smiles at me commenting on how the collar
Caught some blood and how sorry, how stiff

She is, cold hands and worried about me
All of a sudden showing more care slightly

More than I am accustomed to, not being together
With anyone for long, she comments my hair is not white

And what hair remains matches the tortoise
Shell as she lectures that I should floss worries, problems

Away daily, so as not to let the tar and plaque of it all
Build up somewhere else, even perhaps the heart.

# We Always

Debated about colors, if people really saw the exact same
Color. If your blue or yellow was the same hue as my yellow
And blue. These were my first steps toward you and my first
Steps away, the same steps I would learn, you, my daughter would practice
As you turned into teen years your hugs began to not touch rib to rib
The hugs that used to be an expression of closeness, turned now to quiet courtesy

So the disciplines I started and threw up as a father were not courteous
For argument's sake you threw up the very exact same
Sort of words that fail me now as a father who finally longs to rib
My daughter about your crayon drawings on the wall of our past yellow
And blue art you drew and you laughed behind a blue chair practicing
Portraits and landscapes and these were your very first

Attempts at communicating to the world about your visions, your first
Expressions and thoughts that were always more curious, yet courteous
You apologized to me, that you did not know the wall could be used for practice
And my strong bass voice and my surprise still shocked you causing the same
Tears as any spanking, as any yelling could ever do I felt yellow,
Like a coward, because of my reaction I could see your sobs expand in your ribs

And now I stand by this airport window, seeing my breath, my ribs
Rise and fall with impatience and this not being the last or the first
Wait I see the airplanes come and go, the baggage carts with yellow
Lights flashing and the last few people waiting, smiling, being courteous
As I look out staring in a daze the constant looking at my watch, the same
Anxious feeling I have had numerous times in my life practicing

Piano ready to learn the final notes, ready to play the whole piece, practicing

# We Always

A smile, an attempt at getting along with the rest of the world, trying
to rib
The guys at the club after golf, trying to not stand out, trying to be
the same
As everyone else I gave up a lot of me and not being the last time or
the first
It is getting late for me and only a few remain now, the janitor
courteous
As I wish I could get a cup of coffee or see something other than
yellow

Lights flashing carrying luggage around the tarmac the little yellow
Lights zoom in and around the planes as if unloading and loading was
practice
For the obvious I am waiting but you are not landing and I don't feel
so courteous
Because there is no call, no message so easy in this day and age it
sticks to the ribs
This sort of pain as I ask there are no more arriving flights and the
first
Flight in the morning is not coming from where you now live, no it is
the same

As tonight, tomorrow I will practice piano at home first thing and
sing, filling my ribs
With the bass notes the same way I did years ago, not courteous
enough to realize the same
Yellow colors of you are the definitions of distance, started long ago
with a serve of words.

# Potting Pines

On my back porch I take a break and jerk the dead tomato plants
Out of my summer garden, they come easy this warm November afternoon
A few hard green tomatoes left I pitch the plants down by the pond
Where frogs still sun themselves ready to return next March or April
The dogs play with the few hard green tomatoes I toss them like small
Tennis balls these green globes become the dogs' world, their entertainment

In the winter sun I continue to pot the pines, this my entertainment,
Taking my time I start counting and there must be at least forty plants
Which I plan will form a wall in twenty years because now they are small
But by then I will want more seclusion and not have this energy in the afternoon
I imagine myself writing and reading and looking forward to each April
I live I think the north side of my property will be best, near the pond

The wall will keep me blocked off from any new houses built near the pond
Where the frogs, fish, and fowl will keep me company and entertained
I think how easily the tomato plants were uprooted, and how in April
When I planted them the clumps of soil clung to the roots of the plants
That looked so depressed, like small trees not quite belonging to the afternoon
Dusk comes on and I question the soil clinging to the roots to life so small

Their roots bore hundreds of tomatoes all summer only to leave a few small
Ones unlike the catfish and bass I am catching late in the season out of the pond
The last part of life before hibernation and these plants, this planting, this afternoon,
This continuation like the black hose, a long snake weaving and entertaining
The dogs I pull it out of the garden, it is under the leaves, the other plants
As if it was hiding, slithering like the cats as they scurry across the porch, across April

I recall how I worked hard tilling the black earth, the cats purring all across April

# Potting Pines

I marked the days off the calendar anxious to see the first signs of any small
Budding yellow flower indicating tomatoes would soon follow on the young plants
As the cats followed my ankles feeding me attention as they did by the pond
All summer as I fished they were anxious for any fish I landed, entertained
With the flopping of fins on the bank, I unhooked as they jumped at the afternoon

And this is how I spend my days and my long, long simple afternoons
With oncoming nights and the gentle worship from my dogs, recalling April
And my cats' adoration and how sad this sort of quiet entertainment
Introduces me back to the very reason I moved and live here is this small
Pond and the geese and the ducks coming and going, landing on the pond
And taking off into the air like I used to on various flights, but now I plant

And catch, the only catch is oncoming darkness, so I hurriedly pot pines, small
Young plants, the afternoon gone and the potting table black with spilled soil, the pond
Catching the last part of any light as I entertain thoughts of borders and future Aprils.

# Sunday Morning

Our cat kills a tufted titmouse
My fault because I didn't feed
The cat but late yesterday afternoon
I poured bird food and the feeder

Too heavy, too low made for easy
Prey outside but here in the quiet
Of the sun room the dogs' barking
On the far side of our property

Wakes you up and you complain
Of a headache and that we have to hurry
To make church and that you are hungry
I get up from my couch bed looking

Again at the headless bird our cat
Begs, cries for food on the other side
Of the glass the wings are scattered
Over the fresh fallen snow on the porch

The grey feathers look like ashes
The same color as my hands that built
Our first fire of the season last night
I checked out the flue with a flashlight

To be sure it was clear that nothing
Tragic would happen around our home.

# Body Releases
# Or So Many Buffet Choices

Vomit. Crap. Piss. Sneeze. Bleed. Spit
Orgasm. Slowly sweating, rising, oozing squirt.

Loosing teeth enamel and hair, the color of each
Is that some ear wax dropping out of my ear?

Some puss in that little pimple on my chin?
Regardless I am hearing you really want in?

Regardless of blemishes or bruises these tears accept
The years of waste and skin that have been peeled

Yet I fart and burp and pick my nose
And you shop in aisles of men and coughing,

Almost choking still say you want one of those
The one being me and I am

Now yours breathing in and out
Heartbeat without a yawn.

# Frame 8072007: Luck Would Have It

Two weeks ago today I had two drug coated stents put in my left
anterior descending artery

One of the big ones. Today I walked three miles in an oncoming
thunderstorm no longer afraid.

Today is garbage day in Northeast Ohio and I witness how we
consume so much and dispose

Of it weekly in our pop, beer, potato chip, diaper world we gobble
oxygen and water and oil.

In my right hand I notice the veins and arteries are more pronounced
now close to the way

They were in my youth when I put my arms around yearning girls
looking for love the way

I did and do life now. The only meaning I have found here is love and
words. Words to express

What I am feeling and thinking. And for love, the ultimate falling into
and out of and back again.

Other than this I find the world a silly place. One where I am
compelled to write what I see

However slanted or biased it is based on my own traumas. Perhaps this
is why I have never

Had a real shot at happiness. I have from such an early age been more
the victim than the victor.

# Frame 8072007: Luck Would Have It (continued)

Not that there is much glory in victory, since it is so short lived. My victory is the love and life and

The words. Scribbles at paper, reaches for skin. No longer caught up in the have to or must do

I tell you these things since I walk among thunder and lightning. No longer afraid. Death on the run.

# Soul Pain

Sometimes you wake up and you know why
Something is bothering you and you know what it is

You wish it would stop or go away or you could avoid it
But like a shadow when there is light enough it is there

So you wish for darkness and walk into darkness sure
There will be nothing that will follow you there

Wooden bridges in the Virginia mountains echo your
Footsteps and only an owl or whatever night animal

You share this darkness with knows you are here
But they don't care because they are hunting like you

Hungry for something and trying to fill an appetite
They do not trust yet they do not question

So the waters belong to your soul as they run by you
Under your feet you hear them but barely can see

Their depths because of this darkness, this darkness
You have come to love instead of someone

And this is where you wander aimlessly so content
That you forget why you started out or how you got

To where you are until that one you have heard about
Calls your name and you hear her there where the

Sun crawls up over the horizon her face is in the light
And before you run away you see her eyes as if you were

Welcome to dive into them and swim aimlessly forever
Not afraid of drowning as you are swallowed up.

# Exposed

Twenty years ago I was playing tennis and I went into what they call
atrial fibrillation
And a cardiologist at The Cleveland Clinic prescribed a drug called
Tambocor for me

To take twice a day and after that pretty much my life was normal, oh
I had an occasional
Missed beat or two or even once in a bit I had a run of skipped beats
but I ran, swam,

Biked, water and snow skied and snorkeled my way through Caribbean
waters and Women's tan legs and never had any problems. I recall Dr.
Maloney telling me we would

Try to kill the weeds and not the grass in my heart and so for twenty
years it worked
Until my Left Anterior Descending artery narrowed to ninety five
percent and they had

To put two drug eluding stents in and they had to stop the Tambocor
because it is very
Deadly or been shown to be in patients with stents and by-pass and
heart attacks and so

Here I am twenty years later and who knows where Maloney is but my
new English
Cardiologist knew him well and said we would make a go of it without
the Tambocor and

See if my atrial fibrillation comes back or it did kill the weeds after all
these years and of
Course this is OK by me as long as it doesn't come back. That's a fact
Jack.

Bill Garten is winner of the Margaret Ward Martin Prize for Creative Writing and The Emerson Prize for Poetry. He has published poetry in hundreds of literary journals and magazines across the United States. Bill is author of three other books of poetry: *Symptoms, Red Rain,* and *Eventually* all published by AuthorHouse.

He has also been anthologized in Wild Sweet Notes, Fifty Years of West Virginia Poetry 1950-1999, And Now the Magipie, a selection of winning entries of the West Virginia Writers' Annual Awards Competition and What The Mountains Yield, a collection from West Virginia Writers.

Bill has lived in West Virginia, Tennessee, North Carolina, Florida, Virginia, and Maryland. He is previously a college professor of English and Business and has taught numerous creative writing workshops. He graduated from Marietta College with a degree in English. Outside of teaching college, Bill's career includes the fields of advertising, marketing, and finance. He lives in Hudson, Ohio, when he is not traveling or giving poetry readings. His hobbies include swimming, hiking, skiing and fishing. His email address is redlol2@aol.com.

Cover design, "Where Are We Now", is a painting by Pamela Tanner Boll from her Dream Series.

Pamela is a writer, poet and artist living in Winchester, Massachusetts. She is credited with being the co-executive producer of "Born Into Brothels: Calcutta's Red Light Kids" which won the Academy Award for Best Documentary Feature, 2004. "Born Into Brothels" also was honored by the Human Rights Watch, the Amnesty International Film Festival, and won the Sundance Film Festival Audience Award.

Pamela lives with her husband and three sons and has taught part-time at Harvard. She is a philanthropist with a focus on education and the expansion of human potential.

Made in the USA
Lexington, KY
13 September 2018